This Journal Belongs to:

_____

Open Letter to YOU!

I'm sorry that they hurt you but don't destroy their shit! You can go to jail for that! Instead, cuss and color their ASS OUT in this journal! Say EVERYTHING that you need to say. One warning though! Don't write any incriminating evidence or if you do, BURN THIS IMMEDIATELY after!

Thanks for your purchase!

Namaste!

Dear _____
(insert swear words of your choice)

(freely express yourself to your heart's desire)

Heartbroken & Pissed Off

Dear _____
         (insert swear words of your choice)
(freely express yourself to your heart's desire)

                    Heartbroken & Pissed Off

Dear _____
(insert swear words of your choice)
(freely express yourself to your heart's desire)

Heartbroken & Pissed Off

Dear _____
(insert swear words of your choice)

(freely express yourself to your heart's desire)

Heartbroken & Pissed Off

Dear _____
         (insert swear words of your choice)
(freely express yourself to your heart's desire)

                    Heartbroken & Pissed Off

Dear _____
 (insert swear words of your choice)
(freely express yourself to your heart's desire)

Heartbroken & Pissed Off

Dear _____
      (insert swear words of your choice)

(freely express yourself to your heart's desire)

Heartbroken & Pissed Off

Dear _____
        (insert swear words of your choice)
(freely express yourself to your heart's desire)

                    Heartbroken & Pissed Off

Dear _____
(insert swear words of your choice)
(freely express yourself to your heart's desire)

Heartbroken & Pissed Off

Dear _____
(insert swear words of your choice)
(freely express yourself to your heart's desire)

Heartbroken & Pissed Off

Dear _____
(insert swear words of your choice)
(freely express yourself to your heart's desire)

Heartbroken & Pissed Off

Dear _____
　　　　(insert swear words of your choice)
(freely express yourself to your heart's desire)

Heartbroken & Pissed Off

Dear _____
(insert swear words of your choice)

(freely express yourself to your heart's desire)

Heartbroken & Pissed Off

Dear _____
       (insert swear words of your choice)

(freely express yourself to your heart's desire)

Heartbroken & Pissed Off

Dear _____
(insert swear words of your choice)

(freely express yourself to your heart's desire)

Heartbroken & Pissed Off

Dear _____
(insert swear words of your choice)

(freely express yourself to your heart's desire)

Heartbroken & Pissed Off

Dear _____
(insert swear words of your choice)
(freely express yourself to your heart's desire)

Heartbroken & Pissed Off

Dear _____
 (insert swear words of your choice)
(freely express yourself to your heart's desire)

Heartbroken & Pissed Off

Dear _____
　　　　(insert swear words of your choice)
(freely express yourself to your heart's desire)

Heartbroken & Pissed Off

Dear _____
      (insert swear words of your choice)
(freely express yourself to your heart's desire)

Heartbroken & Pissed Off

Dear _____
 (insert swear words of your choice)
(freely express yourself to your heart's desire)

                    Heartbroken & Pissed Off

Dear _____
(insert swear words of your choice)

(freely express yourself to your heart's desire)

Heartbroken & Pissed Off

Dear _____
               (insert swear words of your choice)
(freely express yourself to your heart's desire)

                    Heartbroken & Pissed Off

Dear _____

(insert swear words of your choice)

(freely express yourself to your heart's desire)

Heartbroken & Pissed Off

Dear _____
(insert swear words of your choice)
(freely express yourself to your heart's desire)

Heartbroken & Pissed Off

Dear _____
     (insert swear words of your choice)

(freely express yourself to your heart's desire)

Heartbroken & Pissed Off

Dear _____
(insert swear words of your choice)

(freely express yourself to your heart's desire)

Heartbroken & Pissed Off

Dear _____
(insert swear words of your choice)

(freely express yourself to your heart's desire)

Heartbroken & Pissed Off

Dear _____
     (insert swear words of your choice)
(freely express yourself to your heart's desire)

                    Heartbroken & Pissed Off

Dear _____
(insert swear words of your choice)
(freely express yourself to your heart's desire)

Heartbroken & Pissed Off

Still Mad?

If all THIS SHIT didn't work. vou

Dear _____
         (insert swear words of your choice)
(freely express yourself to your heart's desire)

Heartbroken & Pissed Off

Dear _____
(insert swear words of your choice)
(freely express yourself to your heart's desire)

Heartbroken & Pissed Off

Dear _____
(insert swear words of your choice)

(freely express yourself to your heart's desire)

Heartbroken & Pissed Off

Dear _____
(insert swear words of your choice)

(freely express yourself to your heart's desire)

Heartbroken & Pissed Off

Dear _____
      (insert swear words of your choice)
(freely express yourself to your heart's desire)

                    Heartbroken & Pissed Off

Dear _____
(insert swear words of your choice)

(freely express yourself to your heart's desire)

Heartbroken & Pissed Off

Dear _____
(insert swear words of your choice)

(freely express yourself to your heart's desire)

Heartbroken & Pissed Off

Dear _____
         (insert swear words of your choice)
(freely express yourself to your heart's desire)

                    Heartbroken & Pissed Off

Dear _____
(insert swear words of your choice)

(freely express yourself to your heart's desire)

Heartbroken & Pissed Off

Dear _____
    (insert swear words of your choice)
(freely express yourself to your heart's desire)

                    Heartbroken & Pissed Off

Dear _____

(insert swear words of your choice)

(freely express yourself to your heart's desire)

Heartbroken & Pissed Off

Dear _____
(insert swear words of your choice)

(freely express yourself to your heart's desire)

Heartbroken & Pissed Off

Dear _____
(insert swear words of your choice)

(freely express yourself to your heart's desire)

Heartbroken & Pissed Off

Dear _____
        (insert swear words of your choice)
(freely express yourself to your heart's desire)

Heartbroken & Pissed Off

Dear _____
(insert swear words of your choice)
(freely express yourself to your heart's desire)

Heartbroken & Pissed Off

Dear _____
(insert swear words of your choice)

(freely express yourself to your heart's desire)

                              Heartbroken & Pissed Off

Dear _____
　　　　　(insert swear words of your choice)
(freely express yourself to your heart's desire)

Heartbroken & Pissed Off

Dear _____
(insert swear words of your choice)
(freely express yourself to your heart's desire)

Heartbroken & Pissed Off

Dear _____

(insert swear words of your choice)

(freely express yourself to your heart's desire)

Heartbroken & Pissed Off

Dear _____
     (insert swear words of your choice)
(freely express yourself to your heart's desire)

                    Heartbroken & Pissed Off

Dear _____
(insert swear words of your choice)
(freely express yourself to your heart's desire)

Heartbroken & Pissed Off

Dear _____
(insert swear words of your choice)

(freely express yourself to your heart's desire)

Heartbroken & Pissed Off

Dear _____
(insert swear words of your choice)
(freely express yourself to your heart's desire)

Heartbroken & Pissed Off

Dear _____
       (insert swear words of your choice)
(freely express yourself to your heart's desire)

Heartbroken & Pissed Off

Dear _____
 (insert swear words of your choice)
(freely express yourself to your heart's desire)

                    Heartbroken & Pissed Off

Dear _____
(insert swear words of your choice)
(freely express yourself to your heart's desire)

Heartbroken & Pissed Off

Dear _____
(insert swear words of your choice)
(freely express yourself to your heart's desire)

Heartbroken & Pissed Off

Dear _____
(insert swear words of your choice)
(freely express yourself to your heart's desire)

Heartbroken & Pissed Off

Dear _____
(insert swear words of your choice)
(freely express yourself to your heart's desire)

Heartbroken & Pissed Off

Dear _____
(insert swear words of your choice)
(freely express yourself to your heart's desire)

Heartbroken & Pissed Off

Dear _____
(insert swear words of your choice)

(freely express yourself to your heart's desire)

Heartbroken & Pissed Off

Dear _____
   (insert swear words of your choice)
(freely express yourself to your heart's desire)

                    Heartbroken & Pissed Off

Dear _____
(insert swear words of your choice)
(freely express yourself to your heart's desire)

Heartbroken & Pissed Off

Dear _____
(insert swear words of your choice)

(freely express yourself to your heart's desire)

Heartbroken & Pissed Off

Dear _____
(insert swear words of your choice)
(freely express yourself to your heart's desire)

Heartbroken & Pissed Off

Dear _____
(insert swear words of your choice)

(freely express yourself to your heart's desire)

Heartbroken & Pissed Off

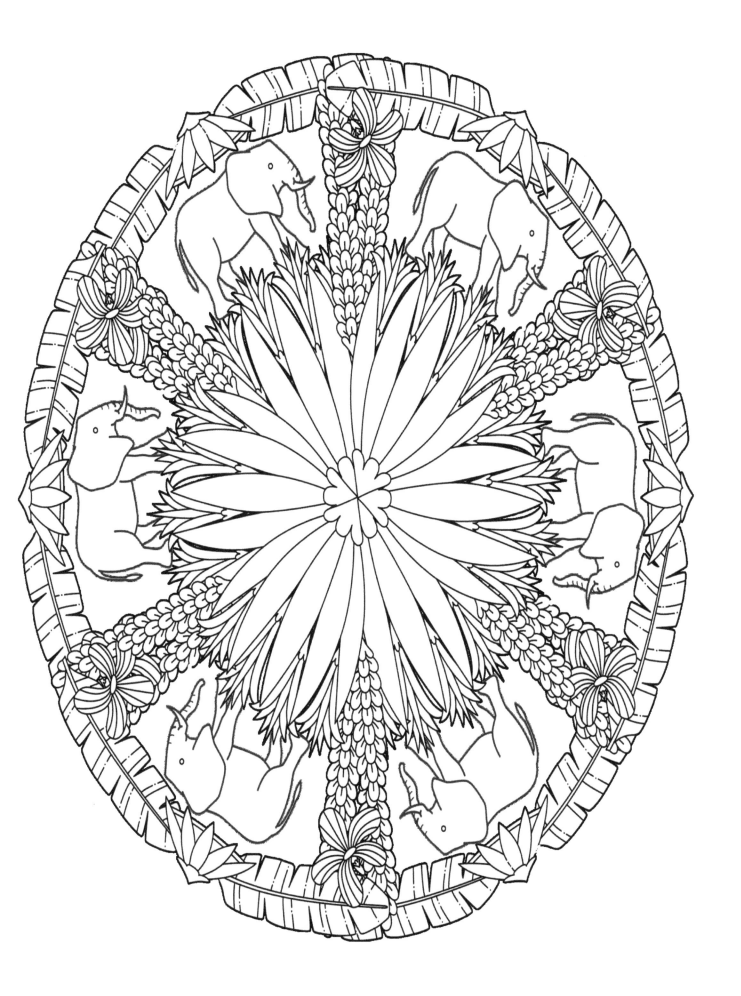

Dear _____
(insert swear words of your choice)
(freely express yourself to your heart's desire)

Heartbroken & Pissed Off

Dear _____
      (insert swear words of your choice)
(freely express yourself to your heart's desire)

                    Heartbroken & Pissed Off

Dear _____
 (insert swear words of your choice)
(freely express yourself to your heart's desire)

Heartbroken & Pissed Off

Dear _____
(insert swear words of your choice)

(freely express yourself to your heart's desire)

Heartbroken & Pissed Off

Dear _____
(insert swear words of your choice)
(freely express yourself to your heart's desire)

Heartbroken & Pissed Off

Dear _____
(insert swear words of your choice)
(freely express yourself to your heart's desire)

Heartbroken & Pissed Off

Dear _____
(insert swear words of your choice)
(freely express yourself to your heart's desire)

Heartbroken & Pissed Off

Dear _____
(insert swear words of your choice)
(freely express yourself to your heart's desire)

Heartbroken & Pissed Off

Dear _____
(insert swear words of your choice)

(freely express yourself to your heart's desire)

Heartbroken & Pissed Off

Dear _____
(insert swear words of your choice)
(freely express yourself to your heart's desire)

Heartbroken & Pissed Off

Dear _____
(insert swear words of your choice)
(freely express yourself to your heart's desire)

Heartbroken & Pissed Off

Dear _____
(insert swear words of your choice)

(freely express yourself to your heart's desire)

Heartbroken & Pissed Off

Dear _____
(insert swear words of your choice)

(freely express yourself to your heart's desire)

Heartbroken & Pissed Off

Dear _____
       (insert swear words of your choice)
(freely express yourself to your heart's desire)

                              Heartbroken & Pissed Off

Dear _____
          (insert swear words of your choice)
(freely express yourself to your heart's desire)

                    Heartbroken & Pissed Off

Dear _____
(insert swear words of your choice)

(freely express yourself to your heart's desire)

Heartbroken & Pissed Off

Dear _____

(insert swear words of your choice)

(freely express yourself to your heart's desire)

Heartbroken & Pissed Off

Dear _____
(insert swear words of your choice)

(freely express yourself to your heart's desire)

Heartbroken & Pissed Off

Dear _____
(insert swear words of your choice)

(freely express yourself to your heart's desire)

Heartbroken & Pissed Off

Dear _____
(insert swear words of your choice)

(freely express yourself to your heart's desire)

Heartbroken & Pissed Off

Dear _____
         (insert swear words of your choice)
(freely express yourself to your heart's desire)

                              Heartbroken & Pissed Off